Author's Note

At Christian Cottage, we are dedicated to bringing others to Christ. Our purpose is to provide easily prepared lessons and activities to teach and engage children in bible topics and discussions. We are dedicated to making bible learning engaging and purposeful. We want to share the bible messages with all seeking His good grace.

Use these lessons in Children's Church, Sunday School, Youth Retreats, in your home, or any other place you teach the Bible.

These lessons were created by highly qualified and experienced teachers. It includes captivating lesson plans, activities for all abilities and children, suggested songs, and so much more. Thank you for letting us be a part of your bible teaching.

Find more books, lessons and activities:
Instagram https://www.instagram.com/thechristiancottage,
Etsy shop https://www.etsy.com/shop/TheChristianCottage,
and on Amazon.

TABLE OF CONTENTS

Early Childhood Lessons

1. Introduction to Parables
2. The Sower
3. Wheat and Tares
4. Wheat and Tares Part 2
5. The Mustard Seed
6. The Leaven
7. The Hidden Treasure and Pearl
8. The Net
9. The Householder
10. Review of Parables

Elementary Children Lessons

11. Introduction to Parables
12. The Sower
13. Wheat and Tares
14. Wheat and Tares Part 2
15. The Mustard Seed
16. The Leaven
17. The Hidden Treasure and Pearl
18. The Net
19. The Householder
20. Review of Parables

Early Childhood Lessons

1. Introduction to Parables
2. The Sower
3. Wheat and Tares
4. Wheat and Tares Part 2
5. The Mustard Seed
6. The Leaven
7. The Hidden Treasure and Pearl
8. The Net
9. The Householder
10. Review of Parables

Bible Lesson and Activity
Early Childhood

Materials Included:
- Aesop Fable
- Parable Maze

Suggested Songs:
- Head Shoulders Knees & Toes
- The Ants Go Marching

Snack Ideas:
- Ants on a Log

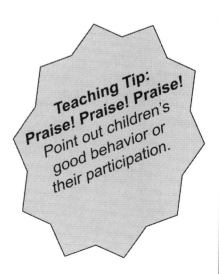

Teaching Tip: Praise! Praise! Praise! Point out children's good behavior or their participation.

Title: What Is a Parable?
Bible Verses: Matthew 13:1-3
Read: Matthew 13:1-3. **Emphasize verse 3.**
Say: Jesus often taught with simple stories called parables. Can you repeat this with me? Parables are simple stories. Say it with me "Parables are simple stories." Let's pretend that Jesus is in the room teaching us right now. How would we act? (Point out a child's good behavior.) I am going to read you a short story."

The Ant and the Grasshopper: An Aesop Fable

In a field one summer's day a Grasshopper was chirping, singing, and hopping about for fun. An Ant passed by carrying an ear of corn back to his nest. "Why not come and chat with me," said the Grasshopper, "instead of doing all of that work?" "I am helping to store up food for the winter," said the Ant, "and suggest you do the same." "Why bother about winter?" said the Grasshopper, "We have got plenty of food at the moment." The Ant went on its way and continued it's work. When the winter came the Grasshopper had no food and was dying of hunger.
The Ant, however, had plenty of food to last all through the winter from his hard work in the summer. Then the Grasshopper knew - It is best to be prepared.

Object Lesson: We learned in that story that we need to be prepared. Jesus taught with stories like that too! They are called parables. We need to make sure we have listening ears to hear and understand parables. Sing "Head Shoulders Knees & Toes".

Activity: Complete the maze of the parables. Explain that these will be the parables we will study. Sing "The Ants Go marching". You could also tell other fables as they color.

PARABLES FROM
Matthew 13

Bible Lesson and Activity
Early Childhood

Materials Included:
- Testimony Coloring Page
- What can I do to cultivate good ground

Suggested Songs:
- The Green Grass Grew All Around

Snack Ideas:
- Trail mix
- Dirt cups (or just bring oreos and let them crush them in a baggie to make it look like dirt)

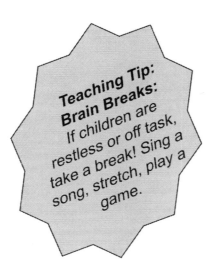

Teaching Tip: Brain Breaks: If children are restless or off task, take a break! Sing a song, stretch, play a game.

Title: Parable of the Sower
Bible Verse: Matthew 13:1-23
Say: "Does anybody know what a seed does?" (answers) "That's right! A seed grows plants. In order for the seed to grow, it needs certain things. It needs lots of light, water, and good soil. Do you know what soil is?" (answers) "Soil is the ground that a seed grows in. Jesus taught a parable about the wrong types of soil."

Read: Matthew 13:1-23. Have the following items hidden and reveal them at the appropriate time in the parable: A toy bird, a glass filled with rocks, a flashlight (to represent the sun), a picture of thorns, a house plant and a cup of good soil.

Activity: (Will need to be prepped before) Make a garden sensory bin. Use uncooked rice (brown) as your base (soil). Add: sunflower seeds or pumpkin seeds (seeds) small rocks (rocky soil) craft feathers (birds) green pipe cleaners cut to ½ inches or so (thorns) fake flowers (flowers).
Let the children play and explore freely. Could do a "seed hunt game" where the child tries to find as many seeds in one minute.

Relate this to our gospel growth. The gospel is the seed, and we must plant it in our hearts. We must have an open heart or good ground to grow in what we believe.

Activity: Sing songs as you color the coloring page. Brainstorm other ways we could "grow our seeds". Complete the "cultivate" page together or let the fast finishers draw or write their ideas down as well.

What can I do to cultivate "good ground" in myself? 	What are some "thorns" that keep me from listening and following God's words?

Bible Lesson and Activity
Early Childhood

Materials Included:
- People Cards
- Sorting Page
- Parable Coloring Page

Suggested Songs:
- Farmer and the Dell

Snack Ideas:
- Wheat Thin crackers

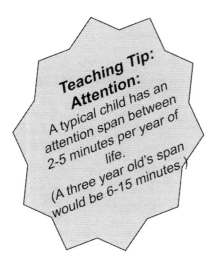

Teaching Tip: Attention: A typical child has an attention span between 2-5 minutes per year of life. (A three year old's span would be 6-15 minutes.)

Title: Parable of the Wheat and the Tares
Bible Verses: Matthew 13:24-30; 36-43
Read: Matthew 13:24-30. (Before reading, show a picture of a wheat field to make sure children know what wheat is.) Summarize parable.

Object Lesson: Bring in a bag filled with different types of weeds and small flowers or plants. Have the children separate the weeds and the good plants. Discuss how it was sometimes hard to tell the difference between the two, especially if the plant had not grown a flower yet.

Show the cards with different people on them. Ask the children to separate the good people from the bad people just by looking at them. The children should figure out that they aren't able to sort them.

Relate this to how we are all on Earth together, good people and bad people. It is not our place to judge or "sort" people.

Activity: Color the wheat and the tare at the top of the page. Sing songs as they work.

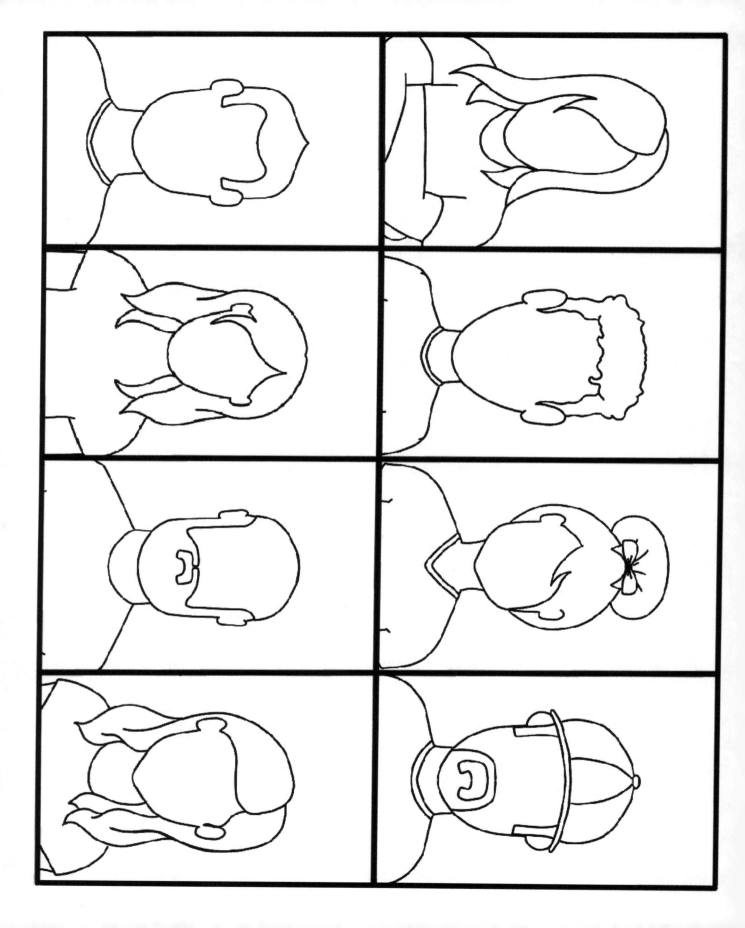

SORT THE CARDS

- Good
- Bad

The Wheat and the Tares
Matthew 13:24-30, 36-43

Bible Lesson and Activity
Early Childhood

Materials Included:
- Wheat and Tare Cards
- Coloring Page

Suggested Songs:
- I have decided to follow Jesus

Snack Ideas:
- Mystery Candy

Teaching Tip: Model! Model! Model! Provide clear expectations for your students and model them.

Title: Parable of the Wheat and the Tares
Bible Verses: Matthew 13:24-30; 36-43
Read: Matthew 13:24-30. If this is your second time with this parable, let the children tell you the story again.

Activity: Pick one student in your room to be the man sowing good seeds. Hand him the good seeds. Have the sower place them on the ground upside down.

Pick another student to be the "Enemy." Give him the tare cards. Have the "Enemy" plant the tares. Place them upside down.

Take a moment to explain that right now with the cards they cannot tell if they are good or bad seeds. They have to wait until the "Harvest"

Then have the harvest. Have the rest of the class turn the cards over. They now are able to seperate the good seeds from the tares.

Relate this to when the righteous will be separated from the wicked. In the beginning they all look the same. In the end, you are able to tell the difference.

Activity: Bring in mystery flavored candy, like jelly beans. Have the kids try to sort out the candy they think they would like. Once the candy is sorted and everyone has a few pieces, let them eat the candy and see if they were right.

If you are doing the lessons in order, ask the children to bring a baby picture in for next week. You bring in a baby picture as well.

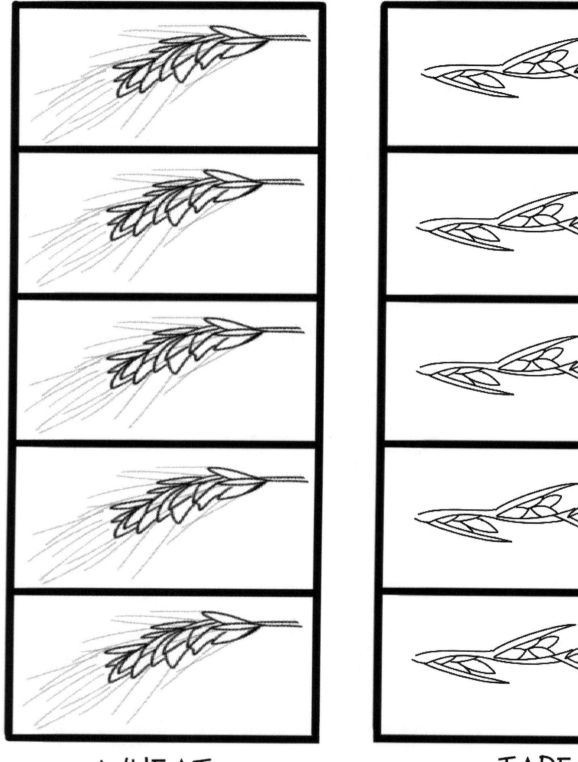

WHEAT   TARES

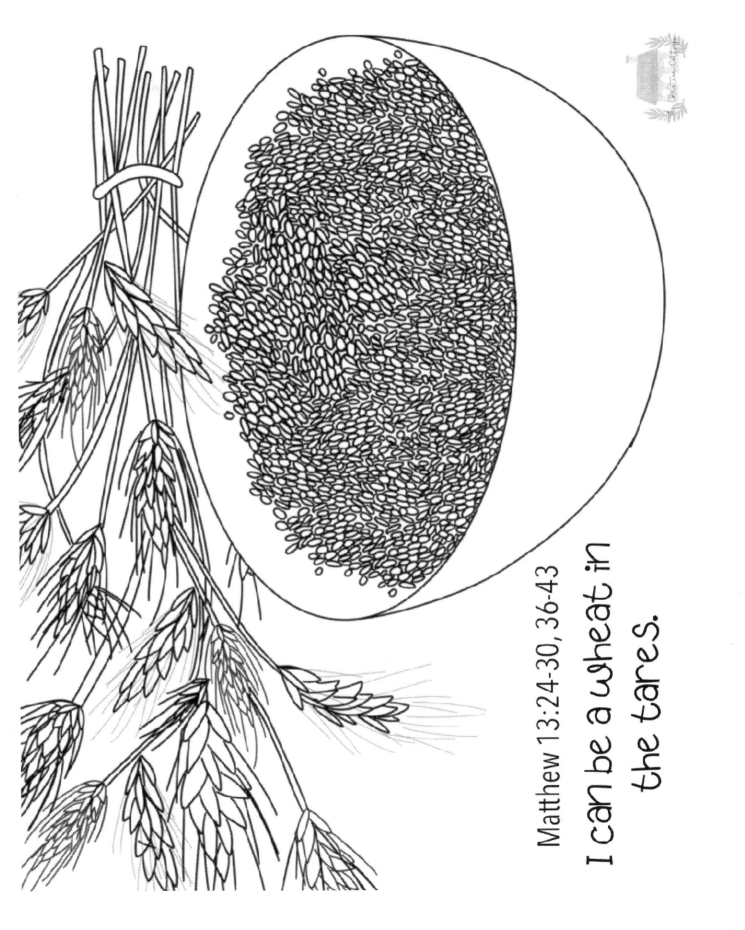

Bible Lesson and Activity
Early Childhood

Materials Included:
- Parable Coloring Page
- Picture of a Mustard Tree

Suggested Songs:
- I am a C-H-R-I-S-T-I-A-N

Snack Ideas:
- Mustard flavored pretzels
- Green grapes

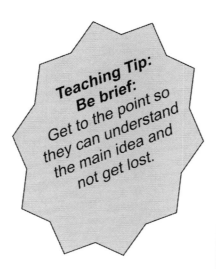

Teaching Tip: Be brief: Get to the point so they can understand the main idea and not get lost.

Title: Parable of the Mustard Seed
Bible Reading: Matthew 13:31-32

Children should bring a baby picture with them this week if possible. The teacher could bring in one as well.

Read: Matthew 13:31-32. This is a great one to read, because it is shorter and keeps children's attention.

Object Lesson: Bring with you enough mustard seeds for each child to have one. Let them feel it, smell it, hold it, observe it, and if they want to they could even taste it.

Ask for guesses of how big they think this mustard seed can grow.
Explain that a mustard tree can grow to be 20 feet tall and 20 feet wide. Bring a tape measure and show the children 20 feet. This will help them visualize how big it can grow.

Discuss how they are small children right now and might not be able to do all the things that big kids or adults can. Look at baby pictures and talk about how much they have grown and will continue to grow. Show your baby picture too!

Relate: Now that they have a visual image a mustard tree, explain that the small seeds represents the church. It started out small, but has grown big enough for birds (or people) to come and find joy, comfort and peace in it.

Activity: Color the picture. Children can glue the mustard seeds onto their picture.

THIS IS A REAL MUSTARD TREE

The Mustard Seed
Matthew 13:31-32

Bible Lesson and Activity
Early Childhood

Materials Included:
- Parable Coloring Page Experiment
- Instructions

Suggested Songs:
- Jesus Loves the Children of the World

Suggested Snack:
- Bread with yeast and bread without yeast.

Teaching Tip: Attention Grabber: Find creative ways to grab their attention. Asking children to copy your sounds or motions can do the trick

Title: Parable of the Leaven
Bible Verses: Matthew 13:33
Read: Matthew 13:33 This is a great one to read not summarize, because it is shorter and keeps children's attention.

Define: Say, "What is Leaven?" Let the children try to answer. After explain that it is a substance that allows bread to rise. Show a piece of bread that has yeast in it and one that does not.

Object Lesson: Have a container of yeast. Explain that yeast is often used to make bread rise. Let each person look at it, feel it, smell it.

Bring with you a 2 liter bottle. Put 8 oz of warm water into the bottom of the bottle. Add a packet of yeast to the bottle add 3 tablespoons of sugar. Cap the bottle and shake it well. Uncap the bottle and place a balloon over the top, show how it blows up the balloon. It may take several hours, showing a video of this experiment would also work. It can be found on Youtube.

Relate: Show the packet of the yeast. It takes only a small amount of yeast to make the bread good. We learn that even just a few Christians can make a difference in the world.

Activity: Color the picture of the bread at the top of the page.

Sample the different breads.

The Leaven
Matthew 13:33

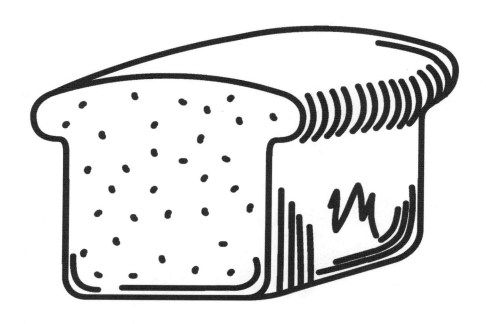

Bible Lesson and Activity
Early Childhood

Materials Included:
- Parable Coloring Page
- Pearl Picture

Suggested Songs:
- To God be the Glory
- My God is So Big

Snack Ideas:
- Chocolate Coins
- Black olives (pearls)
- Gushers

Title: Hidden Treasure and Pearl
Bible Verses: Matthew 13:44-46

Activity: Before class hide a "treasure" box of candy coins or any little prize the children can keep. Start class with a treasure hunt. After they find their treasure, show them something of value to you (perhaps jewelry or money). Ask the children what they would trade for these treasures. Tell them that Jesus taught a parable about finding treasure.

Read: Matthew 13:44-46 This is a great one to read not summarize, because it is shorter and keeps children's attention.

Relate: The man in the story gave up all of his things for the pearl. Show the picture of the pearl and talk about its value. Explain that the treasure in the story is the Kingdom of God. It is not a place but a way of acting. No matter where you live, if you follow God, you can live in the Kingdom of God. Ask the children if they live in America and follow God, do they live in the Kingdom of God? (Ask about other places). Ask the children where they live, if they obey God. They live in the Kingdom of God!

Activity: Hide the coins again and play "Hot or Cold" to help the kids find the coins. Color the picture of the Pearl at the top of the page. Sing songs and talk while the kids color.

Teaching Tip: When a child needs a break, try different ideas to help them calm down (blowing bubbles, looking at a book).

THIS IS A REAL PEARL

The Hidden Treasure & Pearl
Matthew 13:44-46

Bible Lesson and Activity
Early Childhood

Materials Included:
- Parable Coloring Page
- Image of fish
- Simply Fishy Treats Instructions

Suggested Songs:
- Fishers of Men
- Down By the Bay

Snack Ideas:
- Simply Fishy Treats

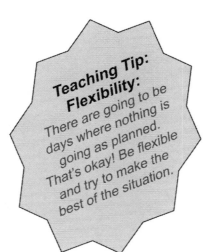

Teaching Tip: Flexibility: There are going to be days where nothing is going as planned. That's okay! Be flexible and try to make the best of the situation.

Title: The Net
Bible Verses: Matthew 13:47-50

Before Class: Have a bin with plastic fish or sea animals. (Tub toys work really well for this.) If you are unable to find plastic fish or sea animals use the images provided. (Put a magnet on the back of the paper fish and make a fishing pole with a paperclip on the end.)

On each fish right a good choice a student could make, or a bad choice they could make. Be sure to have both good and bad choices.

Read: Read Matthew 13:47-48. This is a fun parable to have students do actions to as you read. As you read about casting your net have them pretend to cast a net in. As you read about pulling it up, have them act out like they are pulling the net out. When talking about throwing the bad back in, have them pretend to throw the fish back in.

Activity: Now that you have read the parable, take a net (can be bought at dollar stores usually) and let each child catch a fish from the bin.
Remind students of the parable and how they had to throw out the bad fish. Take turns reading the choices on their fish. Have them decide if the choice would be a choice of a just person or a choice a wicked person.

Relate: Read Matthew 13:49-50. Explain that just as they were separating the good fish from the bad, Jesus will separate the wicked people from the just.

Activity: Color the picture of the Net of the page.

If you don't have toy fish to use at home you can use these fish. Option: Tie a string with a magnet on it to use as a fishing pole. Attach a paper clip to each fish to catch the fish.

The Net
Matthew 13:47-50

Simple Fishy Treats

Jiggly Ocean Cups

- 1 package of blue jello prepared
- Pour into clear cups and refrigerate.
- Top with Swedish fish.
- Yum!

Sea Crakers

- 1 full Graham cracker.
- Cover in blue frosting.
- Add a few goldfish crackers.
- Add graham cracker dust at the bottom of scene as sand.
- Enjoy!

Fish on a Log

- Celery washed and cut to size.
- Fill with cream cheese.
- Top with goldfish crakers.
- Eat!

Bible Lesson and Activity
Early Childhood

Title: The Householder
Bible Verses: Matthew 13:52

Read: Matthew 13:52

Say: Explain in the time of Jesus, a scribe was someone who devoted their life to learning the scriptures and explaining them to others. It was their RESPONSIBILITY to share it with others. Knowing this helps us understand the meaning of the parable.

Read: Matthew 13:52 again.

Activity: Bring a toddler puzzle to class of a farmer with animals. Explain that you are all going to act as scribes. In order to place a piece they have to say one way they could learn or teach the scriptures. As you brainstorm several ways, complete the puzzle. Once completed, explain that the parable talks about a householder, which can mean "master of the house". A farmer is the master of his house and has a lot of responsibility He has to use his knowledge to take care of all the animals.

Relate: Relate this to how we have responsibilities just like the farmer. He has knowledge about his farm and we have spiritual knowledge. We need to share it with others! We spend our lives learning the gospel, it is our responsibility to preach it to others.

Activity: Color the house at the top of the page.

Materials Included:
- Parable Coloring Page
- Puzzle activity Instructions

Suggested Songs:
- Tell me the Story of Jesus
- Old MacDonald Had a Farm

Snack Ideas:
- Animal Crackers
- Saltine Crackers (build a house with)

Teaching Tip:
Humor: Children will say the darndest things! Enjoy the moment with them and have fun!

The Householder
Matthew 13:52

Bible Lesson and Activity
Early Childhood

Title: Review of Parables
Bible Verses: Matthew 13

Read: Matthew 13

Say: "Today is a celebration day!" We want to celebrate everything we have learned about the parables in Matthew 13!"

Activity: Play the Parable Matching Game. Students will cut out pictures and glue them next to the matching picture from the parable. If children cannot remember the meaning of the parable, take the time to stop **reread** the verse and go over the parable again.

Once they have found a match, retell the story, and go over the mean to reinforce their learning.

Activity: Let the students complete the parable review maze as they eat their treats. Play up the celebration idea, you could bring in a few balloons or party hats.

Game: Play telephone where the messages are different things the children have learned about parables.

Materials Included:
- Reflection Page
- Parable Match Game
- Parable Review Maze

Suggested Songs:
- Give Me That Old Time Religion
- If You're Happy and You Know It

Snack Ideas:
- Any kind of special treat to "Celebrate" what they have learned about parables.

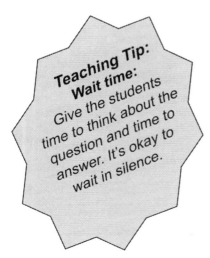

Teaching Tip: Wait time: Give the students time to think about the question and time to answer. It's okay to wait in silence.

After reading these parables I can serve Jesus by...

 Draw a picture in the box above.

Parables Review

Mustard Seed		Glue
pearl		Glue
Fish		Glue
Wheat		Glue
House		Glue
yeast		Glue
Soil		Glue

Parables Review

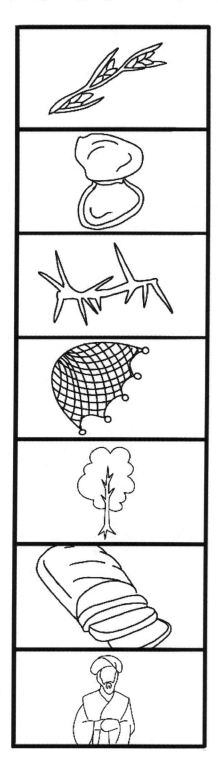

Elementary Children Lessons

1. Introduction to Parables
2. The Sower
3. Wheat and Tares
4. Wheat and Tares Part 2
5. The Mustard Seed
6. The Leaven
7. The Hidden Treasure and Pearl
8. The Net
9. The Householder
10. Review of Parables

Bible Lesson and Activity
Elementary Children

Materials Included:
- Popcorn Parable
- Parable Maze Page

Suggested Songs:
- Popcorn Popping on the Apricot Tree

Snack Ideas:
- Popcorn

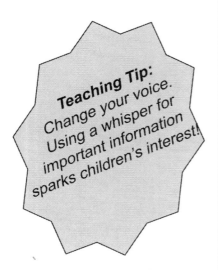

Teaching Tip: Change your voice. Using a whisper for important information sparks children's interest!

Title: What Is a Parable?
Bible Verses: Matthew 13:1-3
Read: Matthew 13:1-3 Especially verse 3.
Say: Christ often taught with simple stories called parables. Can you repeat this with me? Parables are simple stories. Say it with me "Parables are simple stories." I am going to read you a short parable."

Parable of the Popcorn: Author Unknown

Behold, at the time of the harvest, the ears of corn did bring forth kernels which were dried and prepared for the poppers hand. And then it was that the popper did take the kernels all of which appeared alike unto him, and did apply the oil and heat.

And it came to pass that when the heat was on, some did explode with a promise and magnify themselves a hundred fold, and some di burst forth with whiteness which did both gladden the eye and satisfy the taste of the popper. And likewise some others did pop but not too much.

But lo, there were some that did just lie there and even though the popper's heat was a like unto all, they did bask in the warmth of the oil and did keep all they had for themselves. And so it came to pass that those which had given of themselves did bring joy and delight to many munchers, but those which kept of the warmth and did not burst forth were fit only to be cast into the pail and were thought of with hardness and disgust.

And thus we see that in the beginning that all appear alike, but when the heat is on, some come forth and give their all while others fail to pop anc become as chaft to be discarded and forgotten

Object Lesson: Have a bowl of popcorn. Pull out and show the three different types of popcorn (Kernel, half popped, Fully Popped.) Explain that a parable is a story with a hidden meaning. Christ taught with parables so only those with an open heart could understand.

Activity: Complete the maze of the parables. Explain these will be the parables we will study.

Parables from
Mathew 13

Bible Lesson and Activity
Elementary Children

Materials Included:
- Testimony Coloring Page
- What can I do to cultivate good ground

Suggested Songs:
- The Green Grass Grew All Around

Teaching Tip:
Set Expectations: If there are clear expectations in your classroom, children are more likely to succeed.

Title: Parable of the Sower
Bible Verse: Matthew 13:1-23
Read: Matthew 13:1-23. If children are familiar with the story, have them summarize or you can shortly summarize the verses.

Activity:
Go outside to observe and collect types of dirt where you live. If it is winter weather in your climate buy some potting soil at the store. Fill a cup with soil and then another cup with rocks or clay. Use seeds or dry beans on hand. Let the children compare the types of soils. Which would grow the best. Let them see, touch and observe. Discuss which soil the seeds would grow better in.

Relate this to our gospel growth. The gospel is the seed, and we must plant it in our hearts. We must have an open heart or good ground to grow in what we believe.

Object Lesson: Have 3 cups of different types of ground. Compacted dirt, unable to dig up, good soil, and rocks. Plant seeds in each cup. Observe over the next few weeks which shows the most growth.

Activity: Color the page of planting seeds. You may also choose to give each student a "What can I do to cultivate good ground." You may brainstorm ideas together or as individuals depending on the age of the group of children.

What can I do to cultivate "good ground" in myself?

What are some "thorns" that keep me from listening and following God's words?

Bible Lesson and Activity
Elementary Children

Materials Included:
- Wheat and Tare Cards
- Parable Coloring and What We Learn Page

Suggested Songs:
- The B-I-B-L-E

Teaching Tip: Pacing Matters! Going too fast will frustrate your children and disruptive behaviors will start to show. Going too slow will have the same effect! Ensure you are moving through material once children understand.

Title: Parable of the Wheat and the Tares
Bible Verses: Matthew 13:24-30; 36-43
Read: Matthew 13:24-30. If children are familiar with the story, have them summarize or you can shortly summarize the verses.

Activity:
Pick one student in your room to be the man sowing good seeds. Hand him the good seeds. Have the sower place them on the ground upside down.

Pick another student to be the "Enemy." Give him the tare cards. Have the "Enemy" plant the tares. Place them upside down.

Take a moment to explain that right now with the cards they cannot tell if they are good or bad seeds. They have to wait until the "Harvest"

Then have the harvest. Have the rest of the class turn the cards over. They now are able to seperate the good seeds from the tares.

Relate this to when the righteous will be separated from the wicked. In the beginning they all look the same. In the end, you are able to tell the difference.

Activity: Color the wheat and the tare at the top of the page. In the box below children can write or draw what they learned from the parable of the wheat and tares.

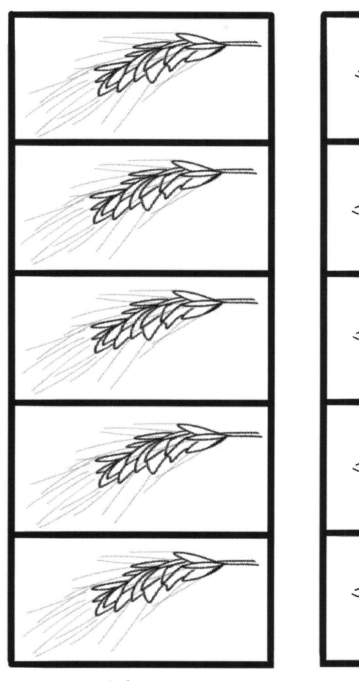
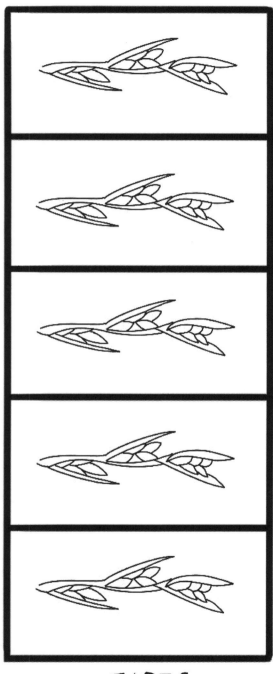

WHEAT TARES

The Wheat and the Tares
Matthew 13:24-30, 36-43

Write in a complete sentence one thing you learned from this parable?

Bible Lesson and Activity
Elementary Children

Materials Included:
- Wheat and Tares Cards
- Wheat and Tares Coloring Page

Suggested Songs:
- I have decided to follow Jesus

Teaching Tip: Enjoy it: If you love what you teach, and the activities your doing, your students will too.

Title: Parable of the Wheat and the Tares
Bible Verses: Matthew 13:24-30; 36-43
Read: Matthew 13:24-30. If this is your second time with this parable, let the children tell you the story again. Have them work with a partner next to them, and retell the story.

Activity:
For this activity, you will act as the Sower first, and the enemy second.

Start by having all of the Wheat cards in your hand. Explain that you are going to put a card on each of the students backs. Tape a card on to some of the students back upside down, on others pretend to place a card.

Next put a hat on and explain you are now the enemy. Take the tare cards around. Pretend to tape the tare cards on the ones that already have a card on their back, and the ones that don't have a card on their back, tape a tare card on.

Now tell them they need to help each other separate in wheat and tares. At first, because the cards are turned upside down, they will not be able to. Explain that at first wheat seeds and tare seeds all look the same.

Now tell them to wait till the harvest. Have them return to their seats. As they are waiting in their seats, turn the cards right side up on their back. Tell them it is harvest time, and to separate into wheat and tares. This time it will be easy for them to do.

Once separated have them return to their seats.

Relate this to when the righteous will be separated from the wicked. In the beginning they all look the same. In the end, you are able to tell the difference. Now Read Matthew 13: 36-43

Activity: Wheat and Tare Coloring Page

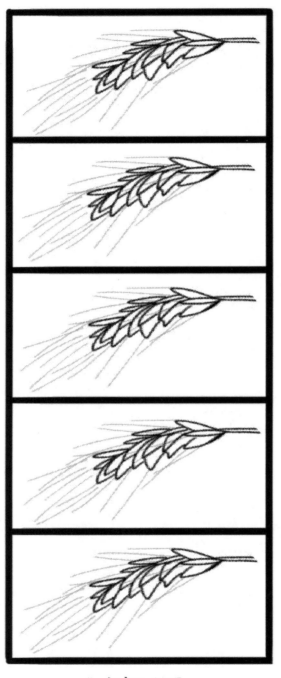 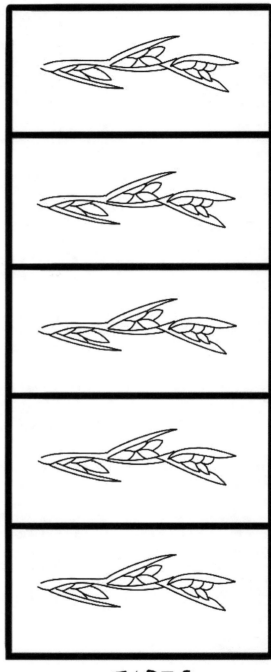

WHEAT　　　　　　　TARES

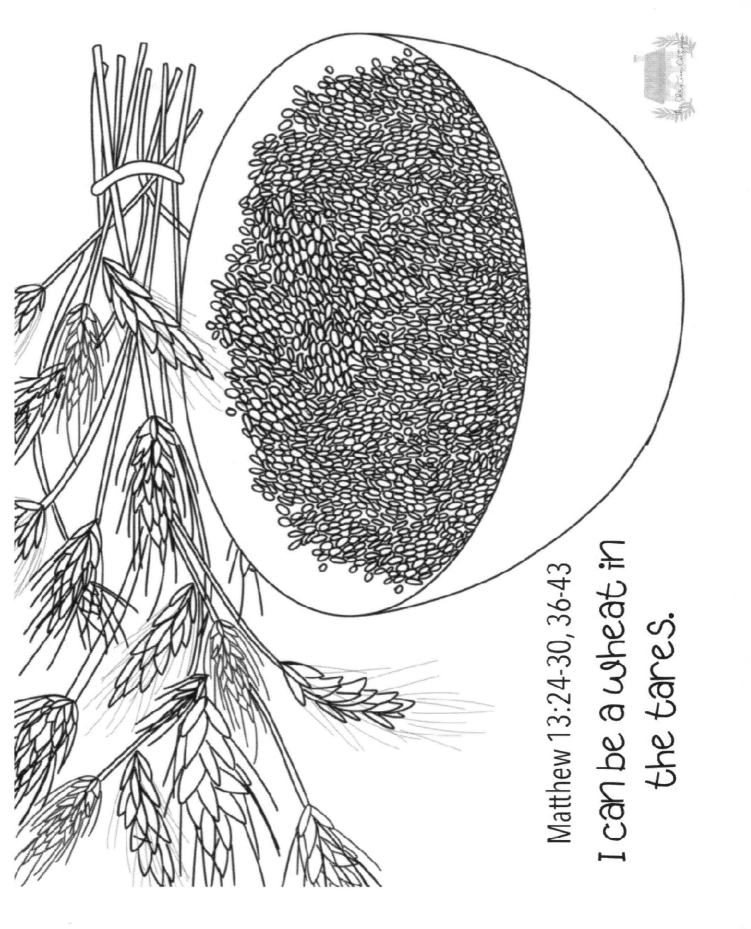

Bible Lesson and Activity
Elementary Children

Materials Included:
- Parable Coloring and What We Learn Page
- Picture of a Mustard Tree

Suggested Songs:
- I am a C-H-R-I-S-T-I-A-N

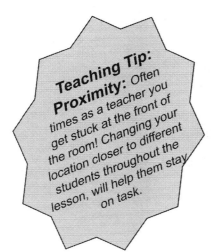

Teaching Tip: Proximity: Often times as a teacher you get stuck at the front of the room! Changing your location closer to different students throughout the lesson, will help them stay on task.

Title: Parable of the Mustard Seed
Bible Reading: Matthew 13:31-32
Read: Matthew 13:31-32. This is a great one to read, because it is shorter and keeps children's attention.

Object Lesson: Bring with you enough mustard seeds for each child to have one. Let them feel it, smell it, hold it, observe it, and if they want to they could even taste it.

Ask for guesses of how big they think this mustard seed can grow.

Explain that a mustard tree can grow to be 20 feet tall and 20 feet wide. Bring a tape measure and show the children 20 feet. This will help them visualize how big it can grow.

Relate: Now that they have a visual image a mustard tree, explain that the small seeds represents the church. It started out small, but has grown big enough for birds (or people) to come and find joy, comfort and peace in it.

Activity: Color the tree and the seeds at the top of the page. In the box below children can write or draw what they learned from the parable of the mustard seed.

THIS IS A REAL MUSTARD TREE

The Mustard Seed
Matthew 13:31-32

Write in a complete sentence one thing you learned from this parable?

Bible Lesson and Activity
Elementary Children

Materials Included:
- Parable Coloring and What We Learn Page
- Experiment Instructions

Suggested Songs:
- Jesus Loves the Children of the World

Teaching Tip: Questioning: Making sure the questions you ask are direct can help promote student participation.

Title: Parable of the Leaven
Bible Verses: Matthew 13:33
Read: Matthew 13:33 This is a great one to read not summarize, because it is shorter and keeps children's attention.

Define: Say, "What is Leaven?" Allow each student to talk to a person sitting next to them (no more than 20 seconds) to see if they can figure out what leaven means. After explain that it is a substance that allows bread to rise.

Object Lesson: Have a container of yeast. Explain that yeast is often used to make bread rise. Let each person look at it, feel it, smell it.

Bring with you a 2 liter bottle. Put 8 oz of warm water into the bottom of the bottle. Add a packet of yeast to the bottle add 3 tablespoons of sugar. Cap the bottle and shake it well. Uncap the bottle and place a balloon over the top, show how it blows up the balloon. It may take several hours, showing a video of this experiment would also work. It can be found on Youtube.

Relate: Show the packet of the yeast, this starts out small but helps the bread to grow bigger. The yeast represents the church. The church at one time was small, and over time has grown bigger.

Activity: Color the picture of the bread at the top of the page. In the box below children can write or draw what they learned from the leaven.

Bring bread that has yeast in it, and bring bread that does not. Let each child taste and see the difference.

The Leaven
Matthew 13:33

Write in a complete sentence one thing you learned from this parable?

Bible Lesson and Activity
Elementary Children

Materials Included:
- Parable Coloring and What We Learn Page
- Treasure Picture
- Pearl Picture

Suggested Songs:
- To God be the Glory

Teaching Tip:
Tasking: Always engage students. If they are reading give them a task or purpose to look for. Everything you do make sure there is a purpose!

Title: Hidden Treasure and Pearl
Bible Verses: Matthew 13:44-46

Activity: Bring in an oyster. Ask if any of the children know what this is. Ask if they think anything of value could come from this. Let them each guess.

Have a pearl, or show a picture of a pearl, and explain that this is where pearls are formed.

Read: Matthew 13:45-46 This is a great one to read not summarize, because it is shorter and keeps children's attention.

Relate: Explain that the the pearl of great price is like the gospel. Once we have the knowledge, we change our old ways for the knowledge we have.

Activity: Hide the picture of the treasures somewhere in the room (For more fun, hide chocolate gold coins with the picture). Give each of them a chance to find a treasure. Say, "If you found a treasure worth so much, but the only way you could have it was to give up the ways of your life now, would you do?" Most will say yes because it is something of value.

Relate: Explain that the the pearl of great price is like the gospel. Once we have the knowledge, we change our old ways. The same for the treasure in the field. The treasure represents us finding Jesus, and changing our heart.

Activity: Color the picture of the Pearl at the top of the page. In the box below children can write or draw what they learned from the leaven.

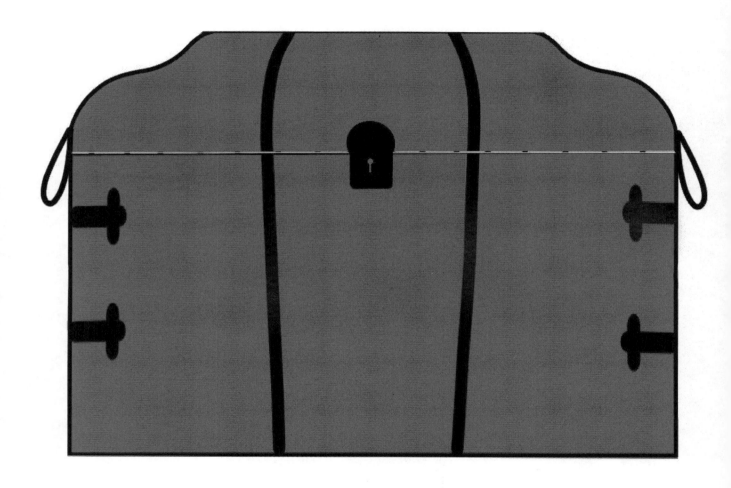

THIS IS A REAL PEARL

The Hidden Treasure & Pearl
Matthew 13:44-46

Write in a complete sentence one thing you learned from this parable?

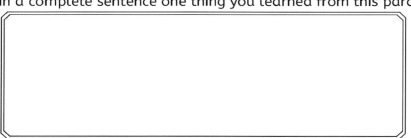

Bible Lesson and Activity
Elementary Children

Materials Included:
- Parable Coloring and What We Learn Page
- Image of fish

Suggested Songs:
- Fishers of Men

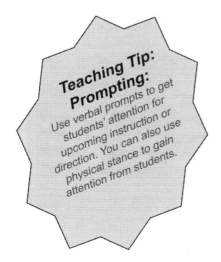

Teaching Tip: Prompting: Use verbal prompts to get students' attention for upcoming instruction or direction. You can also use physical stance to gain attention from students.

Title: The Net
Bible Verses: Matthew 13:47-50

Before Class: Have a bin with plastic fish or sea animals. Tub toys work really well for this. If you are unable to find plastic fish or sea animals use the images provided. (Put a magnet on the back of the paper fish and make a fishing pole with a paperclip on the end.)

On each fish right a good choice a student could make, or a bad choice they could make. Be sure to have both good and bad choices.

Read: Read Matthew 13:47-48. This is a fun parable to have students do actions to as you read. As you read about casting your net have them pretend to cast a net in. As you read about pulling it up, have them act out like they are pulling the net out. When talking about throwing the bad back in, have them pretend to throw the fish back in.

Activity: Now that you have read the parable, take a net (can be bought at dollar stores usually) and let each child catch a fish from the bin.

Relate: Read Matthew 13:49-50. Explain that as they keep the good and throw out the bad, it is like when the world ends. Jesus will separate the wicked from the just.

Activity: Now that students understand the parable, take turns reading the choices on their fish. Have them decide if the choice would be a choice of a just person or a choice a wicked person.

Activity: Color the picture of the Net of the page. In the box below children can write or draw what they learned from the parable of the net.

The Net
Matthew 13:47-50

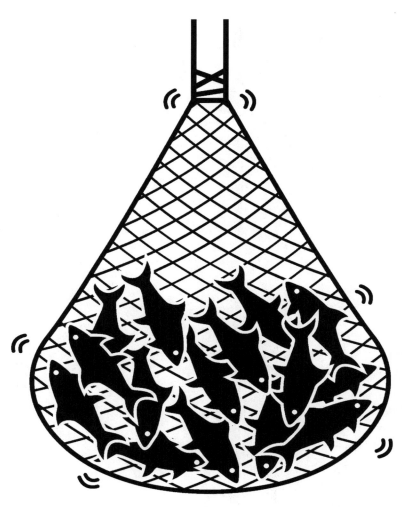

Write in a complete sentence one thing you learned from this parable?

Bible Lesson and Activity
Elementary Children

Materials Included:
- Parable Coloring and What We Learn Page
- Block activity Instructions

Suggested Songs:
- Tell me the Story of Jesus

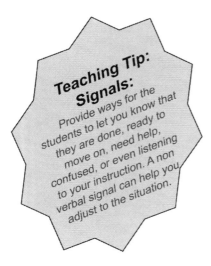

Teaching Tip: Signals: Provide ways for the students to let you know that they are done, ready to move on, need help, confused, or even listening to your instruction. A non verbal signal can help you adjust to the situation.

Title: The Householder
Bible Verses: Matthew 13:52

Read: Matthew 13:52

Ask: "What is a scribe?" You will most likely here someone who writes someone down. Explain in the time of Jesus, a scribe was someone who devoted their life to learning the scriptures and explaining them to others. It was their RESPONSIBILITY to share it with others. Knowing this helps us understand the meaning of the parable.

Read: Matthew 13:52 again.

Activity: Bring blocks or legos to class with you. Take them out. Explain that you are all going to act as scribes. In order to place a block, they have to say one way they could learn the scriptures. As you brainstorm several ways, make the block or legos into a house. Once the house is built, explain that this represents a spiritual knowledge.

Relate: Relate this to the work of someone teaching the words of God. We have a spiritual wealth of knowledge. Just like we built a house each block represents knowledge. Now that we have this knowledge, it is our responsibility to share it with others. We spend our lives learning it, it is our responsibility to preach it to others.

Activity: Color the house at the top of the page. Write or draw in the box below what you learned about this parable.

The Householder
Matthew 13:52

Write in a complete sentence one thing you learned from this parable?

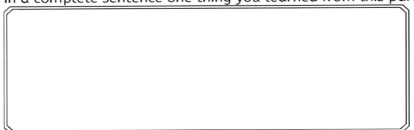

Bible Lesson and Activity
Elementary Children

Materials Included:
- Parables Reflection Page
- Parable Match Game

Suggested Songs:
- Give Me That Old Time Religion

Title: Review of Parables
Bible Verses: Matthew 13

Read: Matthew 13

Activity: Play the Parable Matching Game. Students will cut out pictures and glue them next to the matching picture from the parable. Then, they will write the main idea.

If children cannot remember the meaning of the parable, take the time to stop **reread** the verse and go over the parable again.

Cut out the main ideas into strips. Fold them into a hat and let students pick one. They will read it and try to guess which parable it matches.

Activity: Have students reflect and answer how they feel inspired to do the Lord's work. Then, they can complete the parable review maze.

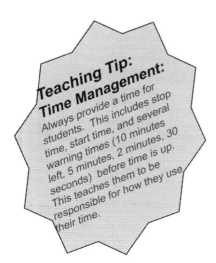

Teaching Tip: Time Management: Always provide a time for students. This includes stop time, start time, and several warning times (10 minutes left, 5 minutes, 2 minutes, 30 seconds) before time is up. This teaches them to be responsible for how they use their time.

After reading these parables write and draw how you can serve Jesus Christ below.

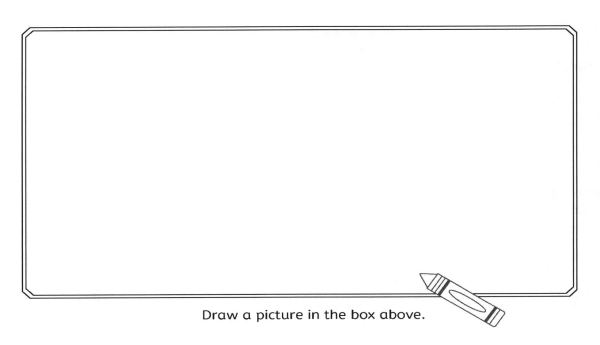

Draw a picture in the box above.

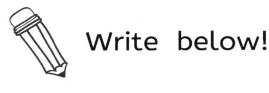 Write below!

_____

_____

_____

Parables Review

			What did I learn from this parable
Mustard Seed		Glue	
pearl		Glue	
Fish		Glue	
Wheat		Glue	
House		Glue	
yeast		Glue	
soil		Glue	

Parables Review

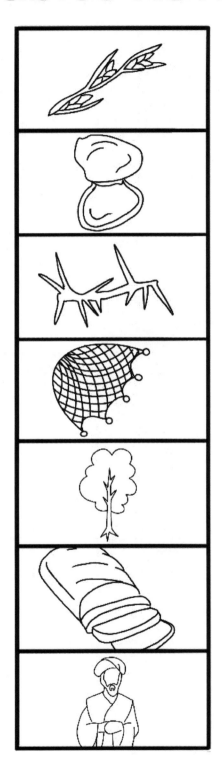

The gospel is the seed, and we must plant it in our hearts. We must have an open heart or good ground to grow in what we believe.

The righteous will be separated from the wicked. In the beginning they all look the same. In the end, you are able to tell the difference.

The small seeds represents the church. It started out small, but has grown big enough for birds (or people) to come and find joy, comfort and peace in it.

The yeast represents the church. The church at one time was small, and over time has grown bigger.

The pearl of great price is like the gospel. Once we have the knowledge, we change our old ways. The same for the treasure in the field. The treasure represents us finding Jesus, and changing our heart.

The good fish were separated from the bad fish. At the end of the world, Jesus will separate the wicked from the just people.

We have a spiritual wealth of knowledge. It is our responsibility to preach it to others.

Parables from
Mathew 13

Made in the USA
Columbia, SC
08 July 2022